HOW TO GET A MILLIONAIRE THROUGH INTERNET DATING!

Dr. Doug Anderson

iUniverse, Inc.
New York   Bloomington

How to get a Millionaire on Internet Dating

Is there Anyone Out There?

iUniverse books may be ordered through booksellers or by contacting:

iUniverse
1663 Liberty Drive
Bloomington, IN 47403
www.iuniverse.com
1-800-Authors (1-800-288-4677)

ISBN: 978-1-4401-5933-6 (pbk)
ISBN: 978-1-4401-5932-9 (ebk)

Printed in the United States of America

iUniverse rev. date: 9/29/2009

*"HILARIOUS AND THOUGHT PROVOKING! AN INSIGHTFUL BOOK THAT **CHALLENGES A PERSON WITH LOW SELF-ESTEEM TO FIND THE DREAM OF HIS OR HER LIFE WHEN SEEKING A MATE.**"*

CONTENTS

INTRODUCTION

I

INTRODUCTION

At seventy-one years of age, I lost my precious, beautiful wife of fifty-two years. Needless to say, I was terribly distraught. I felt that I was old, bald, and somewhat a misfit. No woman had ever expressed any interest in me nor had any woman ever been flirtatious with me. I considered myself a nerd. Even my own father had rejected me as a child. My self-esteem was wrapped up in the charm of my late wife.

Who would want a man with ten children, thirty-eight grandchildren, four great-grandchildren and over five hundred thousand in debt?

Family, friends, and associates thought they had the answers to my problematic situation; but neither friends nor family could bring happiness back into my life. Nothing seemed capable of healing the pain in my lonely heart. What could I do? Who would want someone deep in debt, with ten children, and all that baggage? I alone must take charge!

Ladies and gentlemen, if I could find a mate, who is also a million-aire, so can you!!!

Dr. Nettie, 67 years of age, wealthy, talented, fun loving and beautiful, found herself struggling with the conflict of living alone yet wanting a husband to remove the lonely pain in her heart. How could she ever find a man to replace the soul mate of forty years who was dynamic, exciting, rich, and very successful? Life was never boring as they traveled around the world together, living in luxury. Her former husband was a Cornell graduate who excelled in almost every major sport in college. He is currently a candidate for the Cornell Hall of Fame. He transformed his athletic prowess and determination into the business world where once again he excelled by making over a million and half-dollars annually. How would she find another dynamic man to take his place? Could she ever find true love again?

She dated many men but never connected with anyone. A wealthy hotel owner from California, a developer, A GM executive, a Ford executive, a doctor and many other men fell in love with her, but she could not find herself falling in love with any of these men. The outlook was bleak. Nothing any longer seemed exciting.

She belonged to many social clubs, book clubs, movie clubs, and other private clubs. She was an avid tennis player, bridge player and also exemplified many other skills. None of these activities brought any meaning to her life. Thoughts of suicide entered her mind. Fortunately, a friend recommended the Internet.

PREPARING FOR THE BIG PLUNGE

II

PREPARING FOR THE BIG PLUNGE

"Hello! Where are you? Can you see me? I can't find you! Is there an interested party in the house? Please e-mail me immediately!"

This book was written with one particular purpose in mind. However, it could apply to various situations in life. Its specific goal is to facilitate others in finding the mate of their dreams; whether a millionaire, a love relationship, or just a good friend. The unfolding of this story will give insight into methods on how to obtain almost unrealistic aspirations.

Let me share with you the circumstances that both enhanced and brought a beautiful millionaire into my life.

This is how it all began. Loneliness overwhelmed me, causing me to evaluate the purpose for my life. Oh, I felt I had a degree of success just bringing ten children into the world and being dedicated to one woman for more than fifty-two years. My wife had recently passed away and I now experienced such a void that I could not seem to overcome. Depression was so new to me and it was about to strangle me. Hope was at a bare minimum.

It felt like I was at the bottom of a pit with no possibility of climbing out.

What could a seventy-one year old man with so much baggage do to find a mate; much less a millionaire?

My children saw how despondent I had become and tried to help. One suggested that I shave all my hair on my head. Here was how he tricked me. He asked me to sit down on a chair. The next thing I knew he was behind me with barber tools, which he quickly used to put a clean groove down the middle of my head. After the damage to my hair, my son said to me, "What do you think about that look, dad?" I replied, "I guess I could become an Indian." When I looked in a mirror and saw no means of recovery, I said, "Just finish the job!"

Another helpful child told me that I must shave the rest of the hair off my body in order to be attractive to other women. She convinced me that a clean body was definitely the "IN" look when searching for that special woman. It was certain that now I not only felt like a nerd, but I actually looked the part! Now, I was told that I was ready, but in my heart, I did not feel prepared to face the unknown.

I waited, wondered, and wished but was afraid to venture into unknown terrain.

One day my business partner persuaded me to consider looking on the internet to find a companion. This method would be less threatening than a face-to-face meeting. Following a great deal of persuasion from my partner and trepidation within, I decided to take the big step.

IS ANYONE OUT THERE?

III

IS ANYONE OUT THERE?

This is how it happened. My search began none too soon. I was desperate. I had one problem. I did not know how to get on the computer to join the internet dating. You see, I am quite a bit dependent. My business partner did all the work for me and handed me the profiles. To my astonishment, someone showed an interest by winking at me.

Hallelujah!!!!!! In truth, I leaped with joy, and began to sing! Was I out of my mind? How would I approach this woman? How would I respond to her electronic wink? I simply electronically winked back. The next thing I knew, she e-mailed me and wanted to have dinner.

The big day came when I was to meet with her and I became so nervous that I almost did not show up. Finally, we met. She was very tiny, well dressed and enthusiastic. To my surprise, she did all the talking and I could not get in a word during her conversation. The band was playing and as they played, she kept beating on the table so loudly that I became nervous. This woman scared me because my previous wife was very passive and somewhat old fashioned. I just wanted to go home to my safe haven and rest after this exhaustive adventure.

My second encounter was a lot more relaxing. I realized that my previous date must have been more nervous than I was because of her loquacious conversation. My confidence and courage ballooned to the point of normality. I felt like a stud! I strutted in to meet my next challenge. I stood erect as though I was ready for almost anything. She was that anything! Her attire was so inappropriate that I wished she were the person at the next table, instead of the woman I was to meet. Needless to say, it did not work out although I proceeded through the perfunctory motions. NEXT! PLEASE!

Another wink turned into another date. Would this person become the woman of my dreams? I felt like Leo the Lion! There was no stopping me at this point. I was in total control. Then I met her! Oh NO, not another one! I was out of control once again. She was more nervous than the first date. All she wanted to do was dance all night by her self. She was only content showing me all her groovy moves: what a fiasco! After having a sophisticated, refined wife, I begin to imagine that the new trend was only wild, talkative, non-responsive women. My need for companionship was so severe that I made a desperate move and invited her to my home. Would you believe she kept on dancing and playing footsies into the wee hours of the night? When it became evident that we were not a match, I bid her farewell. I was ready to throw in the towel and call it quits.

The next day when my business partner handed me a profile of a beautiful, wealthy woman, I resorted back to feeling inadequate, insecure and believing that any woman of worth would never have any thing to do with me. After all, the nutty, nervous ones had no interest in me. How would a woman of wealth ever contemplate dating me?

My thoughts were: *"No more women, no more confusion!"*

HOPELESS
FINDS HOPE!

IV

HOPELESS FINDS HOPE

Since I had no sense of self-esteem, I resorted back to feeling like an unlovable nerd who fell back into the same old rut. I was now only destined to be a father, grandfather, and great-grandfather.

All my spare time was spent in total introspection and sitting around watching various television programs. Relationships with women were a dream of the past. There appeared to be no possibility or probability of ever replacing my wife. Every time I spoke to the children about my loneliness and the need of a companion, they seemed to be a bit resentful. Some of the family members felt that it was too soon after my wife's death to even contemplate a new relationship. My self-image was so poor that when I looked in the mirror, I thought, who would ever look at me again.

Then one day while at work, my associate's wife handed me a profile of the same woman who had previously sent me into a downward spiral of self-condemnation. After re-reading the profile, I said to my associate's wife, "Oh, I already looked at that profile." I was gently encouraged to reconsider my thoughts about what I had previously read. After all, my associate's wife was beautiful and she seemed to think that I was an okay guy. Perhaps I was more desirable than I allowed myself to believe.

This time, instead of looking at just physical appearance, and becoming intimidated, I now began to consider what I had previously missed, which was the depths of her inner being. The most important element was her soul! I read and re-read her comments and found her to be an educated, sincere, fun-loving woman, who also appeared to be lonely and reaching out for someone like me. If she really knew the real me, would she actually consider e-mailing someone like me? My curiosity now overcame my feelings of inferiority. What would I have to lose?

Consequently, I sat down and e-mailed her a letter. However, I did not reveal everything about myself because I feared more rejection. Therefore, I did not share with her that I was $500,000.00 in debt. I concentrated on my feelings of loneliness and on the big house that I owned which had a big mortgage. Furthermore, to impress her, I talked about my beautiful 1941 antique Oldsmobile. All I could do was wonder and wait for her reply.

To my surprise, she responded to the silly e-mail by affirming my writing style, my intelligence, and my accomplishments. She tapped into my lack of ego-strength by stating that she was certain I had more to offer in life than a large house and two cars. A new sense of confidence overwhelmed me. Someone found genuine substance in me that seemed beyond my reach. I had never before been able to acknowledge these feelings of value in myself. Tears of joy swept over me that I had never before experienced!

"Hopelessness had now turned to hope!"

LET'S GO
FISHING!

————

V

LET'S GO FISHING

How could I lure this beautiful woman into my pond? What would it take? After all, I lived in another world, on the other side of the tracks. She lived where the big fish swam.

Once again, I re-read both of our profiles to see what language we used to connect. Throughout our profiles, it was evident that music and God frequently occurred. Internet dating had wisely connected two faceless people who shared similar education, interests and spiritual hopes that paralleled each other. The big difference was where she lived, her wealth, and the polarity between our life styles.

So, what would I use to bait my hook? Aha, it came to me. I found my bait! My daughter was a singer and presently performing at the "Tin Fish Restaurant." A voice within me cried out, "Why not call her and offer her a salmon dinner, and at the same time, she could hear my daughter sing?" Was this the right time or place? The weather was certainly not conducive for traveling. It was snowing, icy, and sleeting! Doubt once again overcame me. However, the positive voice within me won out over the negative feelings of hopelessness. I regained my composure and made the call in spite of my fears.

When she answered the telephone, I became speechless and at a loss for words. The gentleness in her voice encouraged me to open up and unlock my hidden pain. My real feelings began to surface as I shared my life story and the loneliness I felt after the death of my wife of fifty-two years. At that very moment, the spirit of fluency allowed me to relate to her how I hated living alone and wanted a sincere person in my life. To my utter surprise, she reiterated the same theme.

When I finally asked her to come out to dinner with me, her immediate response was, "You must be crazy! Do you actually believe that I would drive an hour to the other side of town on a miserable evening like tonight?"

However, after conversing for some time and sharing our hearts, it was evident our souls were becoming one. She took the bait and my confidence began to grow. Could she be the mermaid I had been looking for since I lost my mate?

Had I hooked the big fish?

FIRST IMPRESSIONS ARE

VI

FIRST IMPRESSIONS ARE ....

Michigan always has unpredictable weather as it approaches the winter season, and this year has been no exception to this rule. Today I was about to embark upon what I hoped would be one of the greatest events of my life. I was to meet someone who seemed to be out of my reach. The conversation between the tender, loving, woman and me had touched my soul. Nothing must stand in the way of meeting the one who possessed such warmth and charm. It was so difficult for me to believe that my dream girl and I were about to meet at the "Tin Fish Restaurant". I was so excited, that I questioned in my mind, whether this appointment would take place.

Wait a minute, I thought, as I looked down at my polyester pants that hung just above my ankles. My shoes and shirt were outdated. This attire did not impress the previous dates so how could I expect to make an impression on a woman of means and stature. It would be embarrassing to meet her looking like a worn out grandfather.

There were only a few hours before our meeting would take place. I did not want to panic so I sat down to think!

Who could help me? Who would go with me to pick out clothes suitable for the occasion? Almost instantaneously, the answer came to me. My daughter-in-law had just graduated from college where she majored in fashion design. She and my youngest son lived close to a large shopping mall. They had some free time so we agreed to meet at the mall to buy what I needed to embellish my bald head and shaved body. This was my chance to make a suitable impression. I did not have much cash in my wallet, but there was that seldom used credit card tucked away for emergencies. We shopped for over three hours and came away with stylish clothes that made me look and feel so young. The clothes may have been too young for me but I did not care. I recall strutting out of the mall with a new sense of pride that I had never felt prior to that day. This, I was confident, would be my chance of a lifetime, and I did not want to blow it!

MEETING OF
THE MINDS

VII

MEETING OF THE MINDS

It was almost seven o'clock and I could hardly take the pressure. My heart was racing and my hands were sweating. Would this woman of such finery see beyond the facade of new clothes and have the depth to comprehend the reality of my heart? The nonvisual conversation meant so much to me that I feared when she saw me that she would not see me for who I really was inside.

We seemed to be so similar in both our interests and desires. Our last conversation indicated to me that we both wanted the same things out of life. Family, loyalty, truth, commitment, intellectual pursuits, exercise, nutrition, goals, and religious convictions were so prevalent during our telephone talks. Would this woman be all that I fantasized or would she turn out to be another disappointment?

Shortly after eight o'clock, I anxiously arrived at the restaurant and secured seating arrangements. The table I chose looked out the window toward the parking lot, which also faced my daughter who was singing on an elevated stage. What a perfect scene! The aura typified a romantic setting.

Suddenly the telephone rang. It was she! The adrenaline began to flow. What do I do now? The telephone kept on ringing in my ear. Finally, I stopped shaking long enough to answer the call. She sounded frantic as she proceeded to tell me how she had almost been in an accident three different times due to the icy conditions on the road. To top it all off, she was lost. With my quivering voice, I tried to calm her down.

At that point, she took control and informed me that she was turning around to go home because she felt too young to die on the highway. "Please don't go home," I said to her, "You do not have to stay but three minutes." To my surprise, she went into a rage and said, "What the hell are you talking about, I am not just a piece of meat to size up, I am beautiful." I was stunned! Did she forget that I was a minister and that I asked for a non-assertive woman? I sheepishly whispered, "What shall I do with the salmon dinner I just ordered for you?"

Just then, I saw her circling the parking lot and I excitedly said, "You're here!" "Will you please come in to meet me?" The ice and snow were coming down like a heavy rainstorm. I grabbed an umbrella and ran out to greet her. We both looked into each other's eyes and stood spellbound! Her first comment was, "Wow, you are really handsome!" I looked around to see if anyone else was behind me. Up to this time, people had stated that I looked like E.T. I turned back around, looked into her eyes and melted. It did not matter if she was blind, deaf, or assertive. She actually called me handsome. I looked at her and thought to myself, was she for real? Was she talking to me? Oh my Lord, she looked like a movie star!

From that moment on, our hearts were knit as one. We could not take our eyes off each other all night long. My daughter, Melody, began to sing, "At Last," by Etta James. Our hands simultaneously clasped as tears flowed down our cheeks. It seemed that no one was in the room but the two of us.

As fate would have it, soon afterwards, my daughter, Crystal, entered the restaurant and stated, "Wow dad, your date looks just like mom!" I turned to a man next to me and told him that the singer was also my daughter. The stranger stated that my daughter, who was singing, looked just like my wife. He did not realize that the woman seated next to me was not my wife. What a strange coincidence that this woman looked so much like my previous wife who had recently passed away after a long illness!

The rapport we felt between us was so comfortable and natural that it prompted me to invite her to see my home. Without any hesitation, she followed me to my house. It was evident that this woman was interested in me because when we arrived at my home, she wanted to know all about my family. We sat and watched videos of my children performing at different concerts. Next, we saw pictures of my previous wife at family gatherings. Time had no meaning and before we realized it was almost dawn.

What a polarity between the three women I had previously met on internet dating! Those women only wanted to exhibit their wares with no intention of forming a quality relationship. I felt so happy and fortunate to find a woman of intelligence and possessing so many outstanding qualities.

Then came the storm! She turned to me before she left for her home and said, "I need to tell you something. I will be going out of town for the next week because I made a commitment that I feel I have to complete. My heart sank and wild thoughts entered my mind. Was she visiting another man? My insecurity led me to ask her if she was going to see a male. She would not answer the question. She would only reply that she was a person of her word and that she would see me again as soon as she arrived back home.

My neurosis returned and I became obsessed with thoughts of her being in bed with another man. I wanted to marry her immediately or capture her and move to another island so I could have her all to myself. She could not go and leave me all alone when our souls appeared connected. Did she really feel what I felt? Did she understand how much I needed her in my life and how enamored I was? I must have this woman. No matter what it would take, I was determined to make her my wife. What plan would I come up with to accomplish this goal of making her my bride?

MY PLAN OF ACTION!

VIII

MY PLAN OF ACTION

Dr. Nettie was definitely a woman of her word. She called me the minute she arrived back into town and explained to me that she wished she had never gone out of town to fulfill her previous commitment.

It was now or never! Surely, I could formulate a plan to win over this uniquely wonderful woman that seemed to exemplify qualities and traits that my longing heart so desperately needed. Everything else was set aside as the wheels begin to turn in my brain. Following a time of deep introspection, mediation, and a bit of depression, a thought hit me so hard that I could not escape it! Sure, that just might work! I will take her away on trips and win her over in an attempt to make her fall in love with me.

New Year's Day was fast approaching and there are usually significant events that take place during this festive season, especially on New Year's Eve. A gift, or was it fate, presented a perfect opportunity for me to invite my woman friend to go with me up north to spend the holiday at the "Grand Resort Hotel & Spa," where my daughter, was again performing. A gesture I hoped she would accept.

Orlando, Florida had scheduled a marathon at Disney World

just two weeks into the New Year, and I had registered to run. Maybe she would come along, watch me run and have the opportunity to meet my oldest daughter who lived in an adjoining town. It was worth a try. My daughter and she almost paralleled each other in both appearance and interest. If they hit it off, the pieces to this interesting puzzle might begin falling into place.

The daughter who sang up north on New Years Day, called to tell me that she was to sing at President Obama's Inaugural Ball in Washington D.C. She was in a band that was representing the State of Michigan. Wow! This was almost too hard to believe! Surely if this woman were to accompany me to the President's Ball, she would be impressed and assume that I had a little bit of class, and maybe form an attachment to me. I wanted to do anything within my means to bring about a bonding relationship for life. I was convinced that I had to have this woman.

Just when I was about to present these plans to Miss wonderful, she dropped a bombshell by informing me that she had already purchased a single ticket for a two-week trip to Mexico. She would be traveling and staying by herself in a rented condominium, so she stated. Was I delusional in imagining that this beautiful woman may be off to meet and stay with another man? Was she telling me the truth? My mind began to spin out of control. My fear was that I was being deceived.! I had planned all these trips so that we would be together and create a consistency, hoping that she would fall in love with me and not be able to live without me. Now, if she went away to Mexico for two weeks, this time lapse might spoil all of my plans to marry this woman. It was imperative that she answer a question that would dismiss all doubt about her true feelings toward me. So, I asked, "Can I go with you to Mexico?" It was reassuring when she stated, "LET'S GO."

WATCH OUT NOW!

IX

WATCH OUT NOW!!!!!!!!!

Am I in Heaven or what? She really wanted me to go to Mexico with her. She must have some feelings for me, and maybe even like me; at least a little bit.

The time came for us to head up north for the New Year's Eve dance and banquet.

When we arrived at the "Grand Traverse Hotel," the place was lit up like Las Vegas! Everyone was anticipating a great time. There was an abundance of excitement in the air. The following evening was about to usher in another New Year. Would this New Year bring new joy and long sought after satisfaction, or would there be more disappointments waiting for me just around the corner. I was determined not to let anything spoil my chances of capturing this woman's heart.

That evening the snowfall was breathtaking. If you have ever traveled in the upper straits of Michigan, you would never forget that scene, especially with the pine trees bogged down with heavy snowfall. It appears to be a Winter Wonder Land! My woman friend wanted to treat me at a famous restaurant on the shores of Lake Michigan. The drive was conducive to a romantic evening in the woods overlooking the water. Could anyone plan a more captivating scene than these natural surroundings of God's handy- work?

After dinning at a luxurious spot, and eating gourmet food, my generous woman insisted on paying the bill. Where did this kind of woman come from? I thought men were always supposed to pay the bill. This threatened me by challenging my feelings of self-worth. I felt both valued, and at the same time, out of control. In my chauvinistic era, this was unheard of: a woman picking up the tab. This way of thinking was now introducing me to a new and revolutionized world. Her liberality caught me off guard; yet freed me from taking total responsibility. I had always supported my family of twelve and now I was at liberty to move in this new direction.

On our way home, we got lost in the woods and drove for hours with no travelers in sight. In our panic, we stopped our car and prayed. A young girl appeared in a black van and stopped to admire the beauty of the falling snow. Thinking she would be fearful, she instead exclaimed, "Isn't this beautiful?" We suddenly realized our focus was fear instead of on the magnificent sights surrounding us. She directed us to the next street that led us out of the woods. Our joy escalated on our way back to the hotel.

There was a new aura surrounding the "Grand Traverse Hotel" that evening because I now felt closer to my woman than ever before.

New Year's Eve arrived in a spectacular fashion of lights, music and hilarity. Those in attendance were dressed to kill. I felt like a king at the coat- room as I checked her beautiful black diamond mink. This exposure was not the norm for me but I did my best to keep my composure. Then I took her back stage to chat with the orchestra and singers that were to provide the entertainment for this festive evening. Oh, I thought: *if she would only be impressed!* Next, I secretly requested the conductor of the orchestra to play our favorite song and dedicate it to my woman.

Somewhere around 10:00 P.M., the conductor announced to the entire audience that the next tune would be dedicated to a special couple. He then announced our names. I had never really learned to dance but somehow, the magic of the music inspired me to dance as I had never danced before.

We felt each other's moves and it was as though we were one on the floor. When we finished the dance, we became aware of the circle of all the people surrounding us on the floor.

All of a sudden, it was evident that my woman was angry! What did I do wrong now? She requested to leave and go to the room at the hotel. When we arrived in the room, she began to cry and stated that I had deceived her by telling her that I could not dance. However, she did not understand that I really could not dance! She kept on sobbing while continually stating that I had lied to her. How could she believe anything else I had said to her? She almost became hysterical as she said to me, "I hope you remember meeting a genuine person in your life." At that point, I thought our relationship was over. After a night of agony, I realized that there was something much deeper troubling her.

The drive home had a deafening silence. I assumed I would take her home and never see her again. How could only one misunderstanding jeopardize so precious a relationship? Now it was my turn to cry!

I had procured a book of stimulating questions to engage her in an intellectual discussion. These questions centered on morality and family values. She studied me with a newfound interest. Her mood softened as we moved closer to home. I sheepishly ask if she would please see me again. She said that she would think about it.

ON THE RIGHT ROAD AGAIN

X

ON THE RIGHT ROAD AGAIN

All I could think about was this extraordinary woman! Her memory haunted me day and night. She did not commit to seeing me again; she only said that she would considerate it. How long should I wait before calling her? The Disney World Marathon in Florida was only a couple of weeks away. If I waited too long, she might tell me that she had other plans. If I called too soon, she would probably feel that I was pressuring her to do something that she would not be comfortable doing. God-fearing men pray when in dire straights. So I prayed. I took the initiative and immediately called because God did not get back to me right away. To my utter amazement, she accepted my invitation. I quickly reached for the telephone, purchased two airline tickets, and made reservations to stay at the most luxurious hotel in Orlando, Florida.

My heart rapidly pulsated against my chest cavity and my lips quivered as I approached her home to go to the airport. Her attire was exquisite from head to toe, and a strong feeling of unworthiness, once again came over me. I fought it off by forcing a smile.

It was so exhilarating that she would be spending four days with my daughter and getting to know my family. Incidentally, my daughter's husband was a doctor. Maybe my son-in-laws prestigious profession would raise my level of credibility and perhaps she could learn to trust me more.

At the airport, I stopped to pick up a rented car. My normal response would have been to choose the cheapest car available. What was I thinking? This would be my opportunity to impress her and add a bit of pleasure to our trip. Therefore, I rented a shinny red convertible with all the extras.

When we arrived at the hotel, I was certain that everything was going according to plan. The hotel we were staying in was fabulous. My daughter and son-in-law formed an immediate bond with the woman I hoped would eventually become my wife. My daughter recommended that we see this other newly built hotel situated on the water. My daughter's idea only added to the romantic setting that was enveloping us.

The newly built hotel was one of the most luxurious places I had ever seen. Somehow, we accidentally walked into the executive foyer reserved for government officials, C.E.O.'s of large corporations, and heads of state from other countries. The liaison greeted us and began to elaborate on the services available at the hotel. Her speech was so perfunctory and spoken in such a monotone that it was difficult to distinguish the difference between her voice and a tape recorder. At one point, I interrupted her and said, "Do you think my woman is beautiful?" "We met on Internet Dating and I am in love with her." Then I proceeded to tell her how our previous mates had died, and now we had a second chance. All of a sudden, she stopped and looked directly in our eyes and said, "Oh, my God, I can't wait till my husband dies!" We were so shocked at her comment that we could hardly refrain from laughing. We looked at each other and realized how lucky we were that we were not in an unhappy relationship.

HOW HIGH MUST I GO?

——————

XI

HOW HIGH MUST I GO?

So many significant events occur year after year that both stimulate and stir the imagination. How could a poor boy from the east side of Detroit ever imagine that he would become a part of the most historical event that would ever take place in America? Millions of people were eager to attend this auspicious occasion but only a select few were able to obtain tickets. My daughter was to sing at the President's Inaugural Ball.

I was walking around like a lovesick puppy and one day I received a telephone call that would change the direction of my life. Out of nowhere, the mail carrier delivered two tickets to the President's ball in Washington. I was ecstatic! This would become the pinnacle of my plan to enhance my chance of captivating my woman.

When I called to share this exciting news about the opportunity to go to the Ball, she was enthralled.

We arrived in Washington and the excitement was mesmerizing. People everywhere were embracing one another and a spirit of jubilance filled the city. We were among so many, and yet it was as though we were all a family. Then out of nowhere, the police guided all of us to a safe place because of a pending bomb threat. Talk about excitement! The threat of a bomb could not change the exhilaration among the crowds of people standing together in sub freezing weather.

After walking for what seemed to be miles in the frigid weather, we entered the Ball. We waited for my daughter to appear on stage. One of the attendants informed us that Madonna would soon be making her appearance along with many other rock stars. A famous artist, who did an Abstract Painting of the President, was displaying his work. The music, the art, the food, the people and the events were electrifying. The next thing I knew, my woman friend was standing with the artist in front of the painting having her picture taken. My jealousy and insecurity returned because I felt she fit in with high society and I was only background material. To my surprise, she returned to me and informed me that we were at the wrong Ball. No wonder I could not find my daughter!!!

The next Inaugural Ball represented Michigan. The media, and many government officials were present. The crowd was wall to wall with people hanging over the railing from three tiers up as my daughter belted out her wonderful music. As we looked on, I informed the man next to me that I was the proud father of that singer. He immediately said to me, "She sure looks like her mother." My woman timidly looked at me and smiled. Our connection was growing stronger. I could feel us bonding.

HALLELUJAH!!!

———————

XII

HALLELUJAH!!!!!!!!!

So far, everything was working according to my plans. The electricity was evident to family, friends, and strangers we met along the way. The chemistry that we had and the respect we displayed toward one another were obvious to all. People continually commented about the exhilaration we exemplified and what an extraordinarily charming couple we were together. We stood out in any crowd and enthralled those around us. Each trip brought us closer together, and being apart was becoming increasingly difficult.

Now I faced my greatest challenge! How could I get this woman to marry me now? Life would be meaningless without her. She was becoming more and more dependant upon me, and she would not stop calling me both day and night. It was clear that she was in love with me. Family and friends had convinced her that she must wait for at least one year before committing to a serious relationship. She expressed to me that living alone was troubling for her but she was also afraid to marry someone that she had known for such a short amount of time.

My mind was constantly struggling with the polarity of wanting this woman and my religious convictions. The thought of living with a woman prior to marriage challenged my ethical beliefs. What in the world would I do? It was now or never!!!

Then the big break came!

Mexico at this time was in a state of upheaval. The Mexican Cartel was killing Americans to send a message to the Mexican government not to interfere with drug trafficking. Tourists were terrified that they could not distinguish the difference between the drug dealers and the local magistrates. Many of the Mexican police were being paid off by the Cartel and it was impossible to determine who were the good guys and who were the bad guys! The American government was warning U.S. Citizens to stay away from Mexico because it was dangerous at this time.

This was my big chance because I knew she would be afraid to travel on her own at this tumultuous time. This was the perfect opportunity to implement my final plan. I must apply the pressure now! I would refuse to go with her to Mexico unless we went as a married couple. It would be a big risk. However, I was willing to take the chance. We were to leave in two days and she would marry me or I would not go with her.

It worked! She took the bait!

"All religion, all life, all art, all expression comes down to this; To the effort of the human soul to break through its barrier of Loneliness and make some contact with another seeking soul."

Author Unknown

HALLELUJAH!!!!!

MARRIED

FOREVER ONE

MY WOMAN IS A PRETTY THING.
I LOVE TO TAKE HER EVERYWHERE.
THE CLOTHES SHE WEARS ARE ELEGANT.
YOU SHOULD SEE THE MEN THAT STARE.

I'M CONFIDENT I'LL BE CONTENT
WHATEVER LOT MAY COME OUR WAY.
EACH MOMENT IN HER PRESENCE
BRINGS TO ME THE GREATEST DAY.

THE TIME WILL COME, AS DOES TO ALL.
WE'LL PART IN DEATH BUT NOT BY CHOICE.
WHEN THAT HAPPENS DOWN THE ROAD,
WE STILL WILL HEAR EACH OTHERS VOICE